PRIVATE EYE

Colemanballs
10

A selection of quotes,
most of which originally appeared
in PRIVATE EYE's
'Colemanballs' column.

Our thanks once again to all the readers
who sent us their contributions,
and to whom this book is dedicated.

COLEMANBALLS TOP TEN

PLACE	NAME	ENTRIES
1	DAVID COLEMAN	122
2	MURRAY WALKER	90
3	SIMON BATES	52
4	TED LOWE	38
5	KEVIN KEEGAN	36
6	RON ATKINSON	34
7	JOHN MOTSON	30
8	BRIAN MOORE	25
9	HARRY CARPENTER	22
10	BOBBY ROBSON	17

COMPOSITE TOTAL FIGURES COMPILED BY
THE NEASDEN INSTITUTE OF STATISTICS, E&OE

PRIVATE EYE

Colemanballs
10

Compiled and edited by
BARRY FANTONI

Illustrated by Larry

PRIVATE EYE

Published in Great Britain
by Private Eye Productions Ltd,
6 Carlisle Street, London W1D 3BN,

©2000 Pressdram Ltd
ISBN 1 901784 19 3
Designed by Bridget Tisdall
Printed in Great Britain by
Cox and Wyman Ltd, Reading

Athletics

"The Gold, Silver and Bronze will be won by one of these five."

DAVID COLEMAN

"False start from Darsha – it was almost as though she went before the gun went."

PAUL DICKINSON

"Marion Jones was not flying with all her engines blazing."

STEVE CRAM

"...and I can confirm that that's the fastest time in the world this year for Radcliffe – and she had to do it herself."

DAVID COLEMAN

"The theme of this year's race is Robin Hood, so here to start us off are the Three Musketeers."

PA ANNOUNCER, NOTTINGHAM MARATHON

"Marion Jones was head and feet above everyone."

JOHN REGIS

"...and today is the night."

DAVID COLEMAN

"That was an impressive run by the two English runners – one running for England and the other for Wales."

DAVID COLEMAN

"Backley must be looking forward to the world championships, the title really could go to anybody that's there."

DAVID COLEMAN

"...and there is an empty seat here in the studio which will soon be vacated by Donovan Bailey..."

ROGER BLACK

"Boldon, keeping low as he always does, just like an aeroplane taking off."

DAVID COLEMAN

Boxing

"I don't think you can compare like with like."

FRANK WARREN

"Sure there have been injuries and deaths in boxing – but none of them serious."

ALAN MINTER

Cricket

"To stay in, you've got to not get out."

GEOFF BOYCOTT

"They're very experienced Test players with a lot of caps under them."

DUNCAN FLETCHER

"In Australia we have a word to describe their [the Pakistan cricket team's] way of playing; 'laissez-faire'."

COMMENTATOR

"You almost run out of expletives for this man's fielding."

CHRIS BROAD

"It's half of one, six-a-dozen of the other..."

CHRIS COWDREY

"Once again our consistency has been proved to be inconsistent."

DAVID GRAVENEY

"Pakistan can play well, but they have the ability to play badly too."

JOHN EMBURY

"Umpire Fenwick just itches his nose, rather than putting his finger up in the usual fashion."

PAUL ALLOTT

"…it's a difficult catch to take, especially when you're running away from the ball."

COMMENTATOR, SKY SPORTS

"The spectators are jumping around like dervishes at a teddy bears' picnic."

RITCHIE BENAUD

"The Queen's Park Oval, exactly as its name suggests – absolutely round."

JOHN SNAGGE

"Zimbabwe have done well, just as it looked as though the horse had left the stable and gone galloping down the road, they managed to put a chain on the door."

PETER BAXTER

"Dean Headley has left the field with a back injury… more news on that as soon as it breaks."

PAT MURPHY

"He is like a guardsman. Every part of him erect."

HENRY BLOFIELD

"If we can beat South Africa on Saturday that will be a great fillip in our cap."

GRAHAM GOOCH

"As the ball gets softer it loses its hardness."

GEOFF BOYCOTT

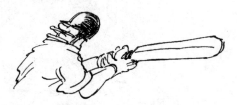

Cycling

"In cycling, you can put all your money on one horse."

STEPHEN ROCHE

Football

"I always used to put my right boot on first, and then obviously my right sock."

BARRY VENISON

"There'll be no siestas in Madrid tonight."

KEVIN KEEGAN

"He's holding his right arm and signalling with his left."

JOHN MOTSON

"I was an ex-professional footballer once."

ALAN MULLERY

"He's pulling off defenders' shoulders and making it difficult for them!"

KEVIN KEEGAN

"Croatia don't play very well without the ball."

BARRY VENISON

"You feel if Chile could just organise, they could hammer Austria nil-nil."

JON CHAMPION

"...at this stage of the season I just tell the players to get points under their bags."

GEORGE GRAHAM

"...of course it's great to see Paul Gascoigne starting at the other team's goal and run the whole length of the field to score."

HARRIET HARMAN

"You wonder if the sands of time are catching up with them."

KEVIN KEEGAN

"He couldn't quite wrap his head around the ball."

CLIVE TYLDESLEY

"And you don't score 118 goals in 120 games by missing from there."

KEVIN KEEGAN

"Well, Harry, fifth place last year, how can you better that?"

FERGUS SWEENEY

"Martin O'Neill, standing, hands on hips, stroking his chin…"

MIKE INGHAM

"…but the trouble last night in Warsaw was nothing like the violence we saw back in the halcyon days of hooliganism."

GMTV

"Is this the win that jettisons you up the table

JED PITMAN

"It's not often you see The Gingerman [Gordon Strachan] with arms crossed and hands in pockets."

MATCH REVIEWER, RADIO WALES

"Tony Banks described the English fans arrested in Marseilles as 'Brain dead louts'. This goes for me as well."

SECRETARY OF THE FSA

"...he's made endless runs into that position."

RON ATKINSON

"He says he'll walk away from the game when his legs go."

COMMENTATOR

"England bowed out of the World Cup with their heads held high last night..."

BRUCE MILLINGTON

"Barnsley have started off the way they mean to begin."

CHRIS KAMARA

"And Seaman, just like a falling oak, manages to change direction."

JOHN MOTSON

"Louis Figo is different to David Beckham, and vice versa."

KEVIN KEEGAN

"I don't want to be either partial or impartial."

FRANK MCLINTOCK

"All the Paraguayan players sank to their feet..."

DAVID PLEAT

"...from that moment the pendulum went into reverse."

GERALD SINDSTAT

"It was still moving when it hit the back of the net."

KEVIN KEEGAN

"They [the Belgian team] were just standing around looking at each other, and that's no remedy for success."

CHRIS WADDLE

"He reminds me of a completely different version of Robbie Earle..."

MARK LAWRENSON

"The good news for Paraguay is that they've gone two-nil down so early on."

KEVIN KEEGAN

"He [Michael Owen] is a goal scorer, not a natural born one – not yet. That takes time."

GLENN HODDLE

"You're not just getting international football, you're getting world football."

KEVIN KEEGAN

"You're on your own out there with ten mates."

MICHAEL OWEN

"And going away from here without full points means the candle is still very much in the melting pot."

ALAN MCINALLY

"The team [Peterborough United] must try to get their ship back on the road."

RAY WILKINS

"Forest 1-0 down... this will be their 19th consecutive game without a win, unless they can conjure up an equaliser."

ALAN GREEN

"I was alone up front, with Danny Murphy playing between me, myself and the midfield."

MICHAEL OWEN

"What's needed at the FA now is a diplomatic dictator."

DAVID PLEAT

"That's the 34th time he's played for his country here tonight."

BRIAN MOORE

"We're in a no win situation, except if we win we'll go through to the next round."

GRAHAM LE SAUX

"A rather pedantic pace to this match so far."

JOHN BARNES

"He'd almost adopted the right position – just half a yard ahead of himself."

PETER DRURY

"So, this movie you star in, The Life Story of
George Best, tell us what it's about."

GEORGE GAVIN

"A great performance from Darren Anderton.
There are those who've had his critics, but not
tonight."

BRIAN MOORE

"That was only a yard away from being an inch-
perfect pass."

MURDO MACLEOD

"Anelka's still scoring goals, and he's there to miss them which is never a bad thing."

KEVIN KEEGAN

"Zero-zero's a big score sometimes."

RON ATKINSON

"Manchester United are substituting Blomqvist for Giggs just to bring more legs into the game."

TONY GALE

"It's not what Ginola does when he's got the ball, it's what he doesn't do when he hasn't got it."

ANDY GRAY

"We had already beaten them 4-0 and 7-0 earlier this season, so we knew we were in for a really tough game today."

BARRY FERGUSON

"Man United now have a home tie at Fulham."

COMMENTATOR, GRANADA TONIGHT

"They've been out a long time; credit them for getting back so quickly."

DAVID FAIRCLOUGH

"There's only one place you want to be and that's Wembley, Old Trafford or Anfield."

MICK CHANNON

"...the problems at Wimbledon seem to be that the club has suffered a loss of complacency..."

JOE KINNEAR

"There was a white shirted foot between Giovanni and the goal."

CLIVE TYLDESLEY

"There's Victor Fernandez [Celta Vigo manager]... just like an orchestral conductor mustering his troops."

JOHN CHAMPION

"All the cul-de-sacs are closed for Scotland..."

JOE JORDAN

"Without being too harsh on David, he cost us the match."

IAN WRIGHT

"One mistake and it costs you a place in the final – one moment of brilliance, likewise."

BRIAN MOORE

"They [the Dutch defence] were still in the dressing room when they came out for the second half."

GLEN HODDLE

"It's not quite as good as Adams' challenge but it's on a par."

RON ATKINSON

"It won't be the first time this season that Michael Owen will be tripped."

COMMENTATOR, CHANNEL 5

"We had a belief that we believed in..."

JAN MOLBY

"The important thing is that he shook hands with us over the phone."

ALAN BALL

"They (Leeds) used to be a bit like Arsenal, winning by one goal to nil – or even less."

NASSER HUSSAIN

"And it's in Brazil's no man's land now."

BRIAN MOORE

"That would have put the icing on his start."

DAVID PLEAT

"The tide is very much in our court now."

KEVIN KEEGAN

"I can take the pressure off the clock ticking on the wall."

KEVIN KEEGAN

"Sullivan stopped everything that came his way... it's Wimbledon 1, Manchester United 1."

BARRY DAVIES

"Germany are a very difficult team to play... they had eleven internationals out there today."

STEVE LOMAS

"...Leicester have achieved a centenary of tackles..."

STUART BARNES

"Once you do go a goal down to a side like Man United the shoulders and the confidence do tend to disappear."

TREVOR BROOKING

"The left foot sees it and hits it out of the air."

RON ATKINSON

"I think the referee should be allowed to blow up now – as a mercy killing, if you like."

RON ATKINSON

"The 33 or 34-year-olds will be 36 or 37 by the time the next World Cup comes around, if they're not careful."

KEVIN KEEGAN

"It's hands on hips and heads in hands for the Charlton players."

COMMENTATOR, RADIO 5

"Michael Owen, he's got the legs of a salmon."

COMMENTATOR, SKY TV

"A first kick of the night for Nigel Martyn, albeit with his feet..."

BARRY DAVIES

"They're the second best team in the world, and there's no higher praise than that."

KEVIN KEEGAN

"Once the ball is at Overmars's feet, it's like a piece of string."

COMMENTATOR, RADIO 5 LIVE

"I know what is around the corner – I just don't know where the corner is. But the onus is on us to perform and we must control the bandwagon."

KEVIN KEEGAN

"If Glenn Hoddle had been any other nationality, he would have had 70 or 80 caps for England."

JOHN BARNES

"Steve Waugh won the toss quite easily."

MIKE DENNESS

"You can imagine the Bournemouth fans with their hands in their head."

COMMENTATOR, SKY SPORTS NEWS

"He just got his body between himself and the goal."

RAY CLEMENCE

"He's like all great players... he's not a great player yet."

TREVOR FRANCIS

"Beattie has made a major contribution to Southampton's performance. He'll come off the pitch and hang his head up high."

DENIS ROFE

"It would be foolish to believe that automatic promotion is automatic in any way whatsoever."

DAVE BASSETT

"Picking the team isn't difficult, it's who to leave out."

KEVIN KEEGAN

"Now Man United are 2-1 down on aggregate, they are in a better position than when they started the game at 1-1."

RON ATKINSON

"We can expect something within the next two days, maybe even the next 48 hours."

ALAN MURRAY

"…and Fulham are growing in confidence now and will believe that they can impregnate this Spurs defence…"

ROBBIE EARLE

"Guppy has a dextrous left foot."

BOBBY ROBSON

"If Walter Smith does not win this tie he will find his jacket is on a sticky nail."

ALAN MCINALLY

"...the ball went over mine and Colin Calderwood's heads and who should be there at the far post but yours truly – Alan Shearer."

COLIN HENDRY

"It's understandable that people are keeping one eye on the pot and another up the chimney."

KEVIN KEEGAN

"It's a conflict of parallels."

SIR ALEX FERGUSON

"The best thing for them to do [Ireland] is to stay at nil-nil until they score the goal."

MARTIN O'NEILL

"We've said it previously and we've said it before."

COLIN HENDRY

"Paul Scholes – the most complete mental player I've ever seen."

BEN THORNLEY

"Football's always easier when you've got the ball."

KEVIN KEEGAN

"When Celtic get an opportunity to go above Rangers they've got to jump at it with both hands."

ALAN MULLERY

"It is better for managers to start out at smaller clubs like Shrewsbury or Carlisle, than to be handed a top job on a silver bed of roses."

RON ATKINSON

"I couldn't really jet off to the States on a whim and a prayer."

DAVID PLATT

"Southampton could well win their first away game of the season, if they can keep their memento going."

DENIS ROFE

"Two late goals, both in the last twenty minutes..."

JON CHAMPION

"Dunfermline have a difficult month ahead over the coming 2 or 3 weeks."

DICK CAMPBELL

"In football, Simon, time and space are the same thing."

GRAHAM TAYLOR

"Goals change games."

RON ATKINSON

"Promotion is the carrot at the end of the tunnel that St Mirren want to be aiming for."

MARK YARDLEY

"Luckily he made amends by going on to score a subliminal goal ten minutes before the end."

COMMENTATOR, RADIO HUMBERSIDE

"Guy Whittingham has returned to the club on loan, and should make his second debut for Portsmouth in the league next Saturday."

COMMENTATOR, RADIO SOLENT

"This pilot move by FIFA will take root and fly."

SIR ALEX FERGUSON

"Dwight Yorke is a very important cog in Manchester United's armour."

CLIVE ALLEN

"That was Pele's strength – holding people off with his arm."

RON ATKINSON

"Manchester United have hit the ground running – albeit with a 3-0 defeat."

BOB WILSON

"Mick McCarthy will have to replace Cascarino because he's quickly running out of legs."

MARK LAWRENSON

"If you gave Arsene Wenger eleven players and told him to pick his team, this would be it."

ANDY GRAY

"At the moment Aston Villa are making a bit of a dog's ear of it."

COMMENTATOR, RADIO 5 LIVE

"Well, that's knocked the sails out of the wind for Inter."

RON ATKINSON

"I have seen players sent off for far worse offences than that."

ALAN BRAZIL

"We are now entering a new Millennium and football's a completely different cup of tea."

DAVE BASSET

"Wimbledon head the ball forward in the shape of Robbie Earl."

JOHN MOTSON

"Historically, the host nations do well in Euro 2000."

TREVOR BROOKING

"As he grows into his size he'll make a very good defender."

GUEST, BBC RADIO 5 LIVE

"You half fancied that to go in as it was rising and dipping at the same time."

RON ATKINSON

Golf

"He [Ernie Els] has just got engaged, which is perhaps why he produced a 69 today."

TONY ADAMSON

"Yes, he [Jean Van de Velde] is a clown – another Frère Jacques Cousteau…"

TONY ADAMSON

"If you'd offered me a 69 at the start this morning I'd have been all over you."

SAM TORRANCE

"Greg Norman has just missed the back right-hand corner of the hole."

TONY ADAMSON

Horses

"A jockey without a whip is like a carpenter without a spanner."

FRANKIE DETTORI

"She ran through the field like water through a duck."

JOHN FRANCOME

Literally

"He had a passion for reading and literally devoured any piece of paper he could get his hands on."

MARK DUFFEL

"There was a lot of physical contact with goalkeepers in those days, and he used to literally kill them."

ALAN MULLERY

"We were literally camped in their half…"

KEVIN KEEGAN

"Preki, he's literally no right foot."

DAVID PLEAT

"Lewis is literally in a race of his own…"

ALAN PARRY

"Paula Radcliffe now literally chasing the clock."

BRENDAN FOSTER

"Every time you pull on an England shirt you are literally under the microscope."

TERRY BUTCHER

"I would never write Sri Lanka off. They can literally come out and set the crowd alight."

MICHAEL BROWNING

Motor Sport

"He [Damon Hill] doesn't know – but if anyone knows, he would."

MURRAY WALKER

"The first four cars are both on the same tyres."

MURRAY WALKER

"It's a sad ending albeit a happy one here at Montreal for today's Grand Prix."

MURRAY WALKER

"He's only nineteen. That's the same age Eddie Irvine was when he was nineteen."

COMMENTATOR, BBC RADIO 5

"There is Michael Schumacher. He's actually in a very good position indeed. He's in last place."

MURRAY WALKER

"Ralf Schumacher speaking in German for our English listeners..."

ELEANOR OLDROYD

"The young Ralf Schumacher has been upstaged by the teenager, Jensen Button, who is twenty."

MURRAY WALKER

"This is lap 26 which, unless I'm very much mistaken, is halfway through this 58-lap race..."

MURRAY WALKER

Music

"The band never actually split up – we just stopped speaking to each other and went our own separate ways."

BOY GEORGE

"…and, keeping the Irish theme going, Sibelius is our composer of the week."

PETROC TRELAWNEY

"We [Roger Norrington's orchestra] gave the first performance of Handel's Messiah on original instruments."

ROGER NORRINGTON

"And that was played by the Lindsay String Quartet... or at least two thirds of them."

SEAN RAFFERTY

"All Chopin's works include the piano, and this one is no exception..."

ANNOUNCER, CLASSIC FM

"Relax. You are in the middle of 30 minutes of uninterrupted music, on Classic FM."

CLASSIC FM

"...of course, Bizet never knew that Carmen was a great success until after his death..."

MICHAEL BARCLAY

"That was the third movement of a Vivaldi guitar concerto performed by Julian Bream as it was originally intended… on a lute."

HENRY KELLY

PRESENTER: It's 3 minutes past 2. This is the non-stop music hour…
[2.19pm, 2.37pm, 2.56pm: Advertisements!]

MAGIC 105.4

Oddballs

"In life he was a living legend; in death, nothing has changed."

L!VE TV

"It's amazing how, in this part of the world, history has been part of its past."

DAVID DUFFY

"DIANA: as the first anniversary of the Parish crash approaches, we look at the impact Princess Diana made in life and death."

PA NEWS WEB SITE

"Damien Hirst tends to use everyday objects
such as a shark in formaldehyde."

FASHION COMMENTATOR

"It's only since I've gone naked that I've got any coverage."

PERFORMANCE POET, RADIO 4

"Do we know what sex the cow is?"

JULIAN WORRICKER

"That was Joseph Weston, eponymous owner of The Cork Street Gallery..."

RADIO 5 LIVE

"Bogey's proving a real handful – he's getting right up their nose!"

RADIO 5 LIVE

"The offer represents a 20% increase on Vodafone's initial bid, but Vodafone may still be facing rejection as hostile takeovers are practically unknown in Germany."

RADIO 4

"The film [the Beach] tells the story of a young back-bencher's search for an island paradise."

JOHN HUMPHRYS

"James Hewitt has caused Princess Diana a lot of distress in her life, and now he is going to cause her even more after her death."

PIERS MORGAN

"Our news at 11.30, a full half hour before other mid-day news."

FOX 41 TV, KENTUCKY, USA

"We'll have to hurry through this, Tom. No hurry, you just take your time."

SIMON MAYO

"If you were in hospital... and you heard that the junior doctor had decided not to resuscitate you, what would your reaction be?"

SUE MACGREGOR

"Of the bisexual men [who phoned a research phone line] only a small percentage identified themselves as lesbian or gay."

ADRIAN COYLE

"Kevin Francis can't help being 6 foot 7 – he was born that way."

PETER RHOADES-BROWN

"...fears that the balloon may be forced to ditch in the Pacific. Mr Branson, however, remains buoyant and hopes to reach America..."

RADIO 4

"...and has bad luck been an element of his misfortune?"

FERGUS SWEENEY

"Sales of the impotence drug Viagra... will be subject to stiff restrictions."

NEWS PRESENTER, CHANNEL 5

"...it's got to be better than decisions made behind smoke-filled doors."

EVE POLLARD

"People's perception of a chairman's job is not the same as they think it is..."

DAVE EDWARDS

"It's like the Somme in here. There's bits of cream cracker everywhere."

RICHARD EVANS

"Survivors of the earthquake in Taiwan are enjoying another night of uncertainty."

BBC WORLD SERVICE

"OK Julie, now pick me a number – A, B, C or D?"

LORRAINE KELLY

"If you are going both ways on the M25 this evening, your journey is going to be very slow…"

BBC SOUTHERN COUNTIES RADIO

"Britain is a tribal society of individuals..."

JANET STREET-PORTER

"That's all for this afternoon… goodnight."

NEWSREADER, BBC SCOTLAND

"Nearly one person in four in the Dumfries and Galloway region suffers from some form of mental health."

KIRSTY TOYNBEE

"One of our listeners will be walking off with a brand new Toyota."

ALLY BALL

"Geri twice told the Spices she was leaving. The first time they didn't believe her, and the second time they reacted with disbelief."

NEWSBEAT

"I don't normally do requests, unless I'm asked to."

RICHARD WHITELEY

"A lot of mail does go missing, and that's being addressed this week."

POST OFFICE SPOKESMAN

"The crowd... a cacophony of colour."

PETER DRURY

"The script evolved after three years of gesticulation."

BILL KENWRIGHT

"The flu epidemic has now reached epidemic proportions."

NEWSREADER, BBC NEWS 24

"We live in a country where children take calculators into exams, for God's sake, so no wonder they can't read or write."

JANET STREET PORTER

"And you both met at the same place?"

KEN BRUCE

"More and more doctors are becoming women."

DR ROSEMARY LEONARD

"My descendants originate from Scotland."

MEL C. (SPORTY SPICE)

"And at 7.10 we'll be meeting the WPC fingered by her own police force."

FIONA PHILLIPS

Politics

"Warm words from President Clinton to Mo Mowlam, she's obviously gone down very well with him!"

ELEANOR OLDROYD

"Portillo will have to protect himself now if he goes for a new seat... And he mustn't vacillate."

RADIO 4

"I think I represent the politically ignorant mass of Londoners, in that I've always voted Labour..."

BERYL BAINBRIDGE

"At least 50% of the population are women, and the rest men."

HARRIET HARMAN

"For the first time in fifty years bus passenger numbers have risen to their highest level ever."

JOHN PRESCOTT

"There's a little bit of Bill Clinton inside all of us..."

EDITOR, SIKH MESSENGER

"The door is now open, what we have to do is push it fully ajar."

ELLIOT MORLEY MP

"Prison... is and never has been a soft option."

ANN WIDDECOMBE

"I would describe the judgment in two words – firstly, indescribable, and secondly, perverse."

DAVID IRVING, IRISH TIMES

"Baghdad enjoyed another night of bombings..."

BBC NEWS

"We're members of the European Union now: if you're a Portuguese window-cleaner, you can now come and clean windows in London; if you're a Portuguese footballer, ditto."

DAVID MELLOR

"My Auntie was a marvellous teacher. She taught my brother and I."

LORD HOWE

"Do you believe David Trimble will stick to his guns on decommissioning?"

INTERVIEWER

"Senior Republicans certainly expected the President to come clean over Miss Lewinsky."

BRIDGET KENDALL

"This is a man [Ron Davies] who has been working his backside off in recent times."

STEPHEN POUND MP

"King Hussein is fighting for his life tonight – it's a battle he seems destined, finally, to lose."

BBC RADIO 4 NEWS

"Some people ran the gauntlet of gay rights protesters, but Portillo went in the back way."

SIMON HARRIS

"Not a single human being has asked me about the selection process – only journalists."

FRANK DOBSON, BBC1

"It separates the sheep from the men."

LORD PUTTNAM

"He's a man who on the one hand is a sinner and on the other hand he's repentant, and on the other hand he's on the attack."

SUZANNE MOORE (ON BILL CLINTON)

"Has Monica Lewinsky blown it for the President?"

SCOTT CHISHOLM

"Bidding has already started for her [Monica Lewinsky] blow-by-blow account."

CAPITAL FM NEWS

"Decommissioning is the perpetual rock upon which we have come adrift."

PETER MANDELSON

"There is absolutely no truth in the fact that I am running to be Mayor of Bristol."

TONY ROBINSON

Question & Answer

DAVE PEARCE: So, pick a number between one and six.
CONTESTANT: Eight.

RADIO 1

GARY RICHARDSON: Laurie, marks out of ten for England's performance?
LAURIE MCMENAMY: Oh, I think a good A-plus Gary.

DENISE VAN OUTEN: So where can you get all these books from then?
BOOK REVIEWER: From a book shop.
DENISE VAN OUTEN: A book shop, great.

BIG BREAKFAST

SKY TV PRESENTER: That was a good performance from your dog, and he recorded a good time as well.
GREYHOUND OWNER: Why, what was it?
SKY TV PRESENTER: I dunno.

DOMESTIC SAFETY MAN: If the flame on the gas stove is blown out there is real danger.
JOHN HUMPHRYS: What happens if the stove is electric?
DSM: Well, it doesn't blow out if it's electric.

REBECCA CARR: Have you ever fallen over?
ROLLERSKATING PENSIONER: Yes.
REBECCA CARR: What happened?
ROLLERSKATER: Well, I fell over.

RADIO 4

INTERVIEWEE: There's a plaque to commemorate the site where the first flying bomb landed during the war.
JOHN WAITE: And is the house still there?
Interviewee: Er, no!

RADIO 4

JAMES ALLEN: What effect on the track will the rain have, Johnnie?
JOHNNIE HERBERT: Well, it'll make it wet.

ITV

DJ: What creature squirts a smelly unpleasant fluid at its enemies?
CONTESTANT: A snake.
DJ: No, I'll give you a clue – it's black and white.
CONTESTANT: A bee.

SIMON BROTHERTON: Well, Blackburn have lost five out of their last six, but they did win last week.
CHRIS KAMARA: Yes, Simon, they'll want to keep this unbeaten run going.

BRIAN MOORE: The news will be on as soon as the game finishes, although nobody in the world knows when that's going to be.
KEVIN KEEGAN: How can you think about news at a time like this, Brian?

ZOE BALL: So, do you have any brothers and sisters?
CHILD CONTESTANT: A baby brother.
ZOE BALL: Really? So is it a boy or a girl?

RADIO 1

DJ: Who wrote Hamlet?
FEMALE CALLER: Er, Macbeth.

CAPITAL GOLD

LES DENNIS: Name a food that you may eat
without chewing.
CONTESTANT: Chips.

ITV

INTERVIEWER: How will Sir Stanley be
remembered?
SUPPORTER: As a "living legend".

BBC BREAKFAST NEWS

LADY TAVISTOCK: I was once offered a blank cheque for this horse.
INTERVIEWER: A blank cheque… how much was it for?
LADY TAVISTOCK (sounding puzzled): It was a blank cheque.

"THE HOUSE", BBC2

ITV COMMENTATOR: Of course, Ruud Gullit is the only foreigner to have managed an FA Cup winning side.
RON ATKINSON: So what's Arsene Wenger then?
ITV COMMENTATOR: French.

ITV SPORT

PUNTER: I'm 43 now and have lost confidence through having so many set-backs.
KILROY: And how old are you now?
PUNTER: I'm 43 now.

BBC1

ITV INTERVIEWER: So why do you paint some things yellow, some things red and some things green?
ARTIST: Because I'm a painter.

CHANNEL 4

ANTIQUES ROADSHOW EXPERT: This bronze of a rider on a horse is stamped 'Made in Germany' – where did you get it?
GLASWEGIAN OWNER: It came from Torkee.
EXPERT: Oh, Germany has many connections with Turkey.
OWNER: It was bought in Torquay.

BBC1

ROY WALKER: So, you're a teacher's assistant. What do they do?
CONTESTANT: Assist the teacher.

ITV

AMERICAN POLICE OFFICER: ...at this point the suspect Benjamin Smith shot himself.
SUE MCGREGOR: And do we know the name of the dead suspect?
AMERICAN POLICE OFFICER: Yes... Benjamin Smith.

RADIO 4

COMMENTATOR: Bob, he won't get an easier shot than that, will he?
BOB: Well, he would if the ball was closer to the hole.

SKY SPORTS

HOST: Which fruit has varieties called
Mandarin and Seville?
CONTESTANT: Er... spinach.

BBC1

INTERVIEWER: Who do you think your music
appeals to?
BILLIE: The full range. Early to late teens.

FLIPSIDE MAGAZINE

ALEX LESTER: Got any children?
CONTESTANT: No.
ALEX LESTER: Grandchildren?
CONTESTANT: No!

BBC RADIO 2

GABY ROSLIN: ...and how long will this hour glass last?
MICHAEL BUERK: Er... an hour.

BBC

GARTH CROOKS: Why are Sheffield Wednesday at the bottom of the table?
PETER ATHERTON: Because we haven't won enough games.

BBC1

CALLER: We are celebrating our New Year today: it's called Diwali.
CHRIS YEO: Wow! You get to celebrate the Millennium early!

CAPITAL GOLD

JIM DAVIDSON: From which Greek building were the Elgin Marbles taken?
CONTESTANT: The Apocalypse.

BBC1

RICHARD MADELEY: What is the capital of Austria?
CONTESTANT: Switzerland.

ITV

MURRAY WALKER: Incidentally, the news is that Ferrari have actually stopped development on their new car.
MARTIN BRUNDLE: How do you know that, Murray?
MURRAY WALKER: I was there when I said it.

ITV

W.G. STEWART: Which Verdi opera depicts the war between Egypt and Ethiopia?
CONTESTANT: Miss Saigon.

CHANNEL 4

STUART STOREY: And Michael Johnson wins by over a second, which in 400 metre running is a considerable distance.
DAVID COLEMAN: Yes, well, it's a life-time, in fact.

BBC

EAMONN HOLMES: So, how long does London Fashion Week last?
FASHION PRESENTER: A week.

GMTV

Rugby

"If I've seen two more competitive players [than Armstrong and Van der Westheizen], I've yet to see them."

GAVIN HASTINGS

"Scotland were victims of their own failure."

GAVIN HASTINGS

"We are committing our own suicide."

IAN MCGEECHAN

"A lot of these guys have waited a lifetime not to win this."

DAVID CAMPESE

"Macclesfield have come out in the second half with all guns steaming."

BRIAN SEYMOUR SMITH

"Hopefully, the rain will hold off for both sides."

L. DALLAGLIO

Street Hockey

"Street hockey is great for kids. It's energetic, competitive, and skilful. And best of all it keeps them off the street."

CONTRIBUTOR, RADIO 1 NEWSBEAT

Snooker

"Jimmy White is known as 'The Nearly Man' of snooker, but a lot of people forget that he's got the second-best record in the World Championship in the 1990s."

STEVE DAVIS

"He [Jack Doherty] won't be able to pot that red unless he manages to hit it."

JOHN VIRGO

Swimming

"The swimmers are swimming out of their socks."

SHARRON DAVIES

"It was the fastest-ever swim over that distance on American soil."

GREG PHILLIPS

Tennis

"I have a feeling that, if she had been playing against herself, she would have won that point."

BOB HEWITT

"Getting your first serve in is a great way to avoid double faults."

JOHN FITZGERALD